GERALD AND HIS WORLD

Author and translator
Robert M. Morris

Cardiff
University of Wales Press
1987

© Crown copyright, 1986

British Library Cataloguing in Publication Data

Morris, Robert M.
  Gerald and his world.
  1. Giraldis, *Cambrensis* 2. Historians —
  Wales — Biography
  I. Title II. Gerallt a'i gefndir. *English*
  942.9'0072024 DA209.G5

  ISBN 0-7083-0969-0

ACKNOWLEDGEMENTS

The publishers would like to thank the following for permission to reproduce photographs and for their assistance.

Cloud Nine Design: Gerald's Age: A Survey

British Library Board: 3(A)

National Library of Wales: 3(B), 4(E) (NLW MS 3024C), 21(R) (Peniarth MS 28), 21(T) (Peniarth MS 28)

Anne Mainman: 4(C), 5(F), 6(A), 7(B), 7(C), 9(A), 12(D), 14(J), 23(A), 24(C)

Conway Library, Courtauld Institute of Art; Maurice H. Ridgway: 4(D)

Lynne Sieger: 6 (monks)

BBC Hulton Picture Library: 8(E), 11(A), 13(I), 15(L), 17(A), 20(O)

Eric Hall: 8(F)

Penni Bestic: 8(G), 11(B)

Bodleian Library, Oxford, MS. Laud. Misc. 720, f. 226: 10(C)

The Mansell Collection Ltd: 11(C), 15(M)

Peredur Wyn Powell: 12(E)

Caisse Nationale des Monuments Historiques et des Sites, Reims (Marne), Cathédrale: Transept Nord, Statue de Roi dite Philippe Auguste, © CNMHS/SPADEM 1986: 13(G)

Mary Evans Picture Library: 14(K)

Bibliotheque Nationale: 16(N)

The British Library: 16(O), 20(M), 25(F)

Burgerbibliothek Bern: 16(P)

Terence Soames (Cardiff) Ltd: 18(E), 25(G)

National Museum of Wales: 21(Q)

Public Record Office: 22(V)

Ray Daniel: 26(H)

Ronald Sheridan's Photo-Library: 27(J)

CONTENTS

The Age of Gerald: A Survey 2
1. Introduction 4
2. Wales in Gerald's Time 7
3. The Invasion of Ireland 10
4. Gerald and the Crown 12
5. Gerald's View of Wales 18
6. Gerald and his Church 23
7. Glossary 28

TIME-CHART OF MAIN EVENTS

1164 Henry II flees from the Berwyn
1169 Normans invade Ireland
1170 Thomas à Becket murdered
1176 Cardigan Eisteddfod
1187 Turks invade Jerusalem
1188 Gerald campaigns for the crusades
1189 The King dies in France
1193 Richard III missing in Austria
1197 The Lord Rhys dies
1215 John signs Magna Carter
1223 Gerald of Wales dies

All rights reserved. No part of this book may be reproduced, stored in a retrieval system, or transmitted, in any form or by any means, electronic, mechanical, photocopying, recording or otherwise, without clearance from the University of Wales Press, 6 Gwennyth Street, Cathays, Cardiff CF2 4YD.

This book is based on an original Welsh title, *Gerallt a'i Gefndir*.

Printed in Wales by Graham Harcourt (Printers) Ltd., Swansea.

SYLVESTER GIRALDUS CAMBRENSIS.

GERALD'S AGE : A SURVEY

THE POPES IN ROME

Honorius II	1124-1130
Innocent II	1130-1143
Celestine II	1143-1144
Lucius II	1144-1145
Eugenius III	1145-1153
Anastasius IV	1153-1154
Adrian IV	1155-1159
Alexander III	1159-1181
Lucius III	1181-1185
Urban III	1185-1187
Gregorius VIII	1187
Clement III	1187-1191
Celestine III	1191-1198
Innocent III	1198-1216
Honorius III	1216-1227

BISHOPS OF ST DAVID'S

Bernard	1116-1147
David Fitzgerald	1147-1176
Peter de Leia	1176-1198
Gerald of Wales's Campaign	1198-1203
Geoffrey of Henlaw	1203-1215
Iorwerth	1215-1229

KINGS OF ENGLAND

Stephen	1135-1154
Henry II	1154-1189
Richard I	1189-1199
John	1199-1216
Henry III	1216-1272

LORDS OF DEHEUBARTH

Cadell ap Gruffudd	} 1137-1155
Maredudd ap Gruffudd	
Rhys ap Gruffudd	
Rhys ap Gruffudd (Lord Rhys)	1155-1197
Civil War	1197-1201
Maelgwyn ap Rhys	} 1201-1231
Rhys Grug	

THE PRINCES OF GWYNEDD

Owain Gwynedd	1137-1170
Civil War	1170-1174
Rhodri ap Owain	} 1174-1194
Dafydd ap Owain	
Gruffudd ap Cynan	
Maredudd ap Cynan	
Gruffudd ap Cynan	} 1194-1201
Maredudd ap Cynan	
Llywelyn ap Iorwerth	
Llywelyn ap Iorwerth	1201-1240

ARCHBISHOPS OF CANTERBURY

Theobald	1139-1162
Thomas à Becket	1162-1170
Richard	1174-1185
Baldwin	1185-1190
Hubert Walter	1193-1205
Stephen Langton	1207-1228

1. INTRODUCTION

A British Library Reading Room.

What's the difference between a book and a meat pie? You don't know? Then you're not the person to be running a library or a meat shop! Have you been to a library recently? Perhaps you've borrowed a book from your local library, or browsed among the shelves in the school library? Picture A shows part of one very special library — the largest in the world. This is the British Library in London. It has a collection of 15 million books.

There are 40,000 volumes of manuscripts and three million printed books in the National Library of Wales, Aberystwyth B, among them some of the oldest books in the Welsh language. Think of all the books in your classroom, in the local library, in your own home and in the nearby bookshops. Try to imagine all the knowledge, all the information about all sorts of things that you could find in them. It would be a huge task. Perhaps an easier task would be to find out how many different sections there are in the school library.

Eight hundred years ago things were very different. Books were very scarce and producing a book took a long time. Every word had to be written carefully by hand, and the whole book rewritten to obtain a new copy. A pen was needed for this work. A quill or a bird's long tail or wing feather, was normally used. Books could not be printed as they are today. Picture C shows a man writing a book in the Middle Ages. What do you think this man's **profession** was?

B National Library of Wales.

C Writing a book in the Middle Ages.

In those days only churchmen — monks, very often — would be accustomed to writing. Libraries were usually found in monasteries or churches, and picture D shows how rare and how valuable each book was thought to be. What is unusual about the books in the picture?

D Chained library.

It would take many years for a monk to make a complete copy of the Bible, and quite a while to copy out a **Psalter** or a Mass Book. In picture E you can see the careful decoration that would adorn a manuscript — in this case part of a book by Gerald of Wales, the main character in this story. What has been decorated on this manuscript page? Why do you think the copyist did this?

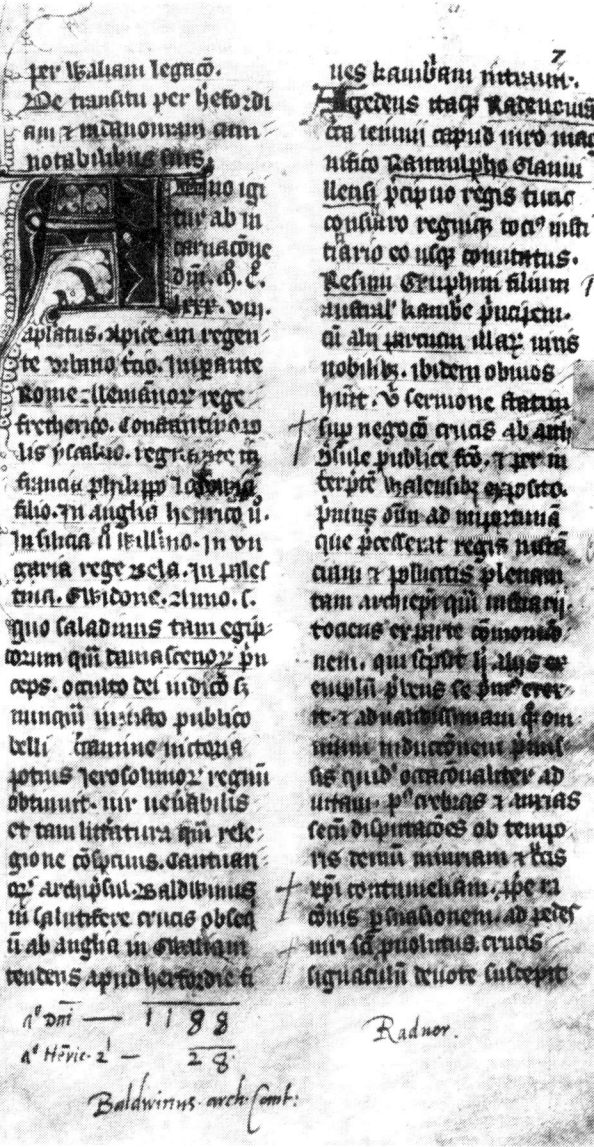

E A page from *Itinerarium Kambriae* by Gerald of Wales.

It was usually monks too who kept lists or annals of important events — the chronicles. Some of these were written in Wales, and some copies were made in the Welsh language. The most famous is 'Brut y Tywysogyon' (The History of the Princes), and copies of it date from the late fourteenth century. The 'Brut' tells the violent story of Wales from AD 680 to 1282. Picture F shows how a book would be bound in the Middle Ages.

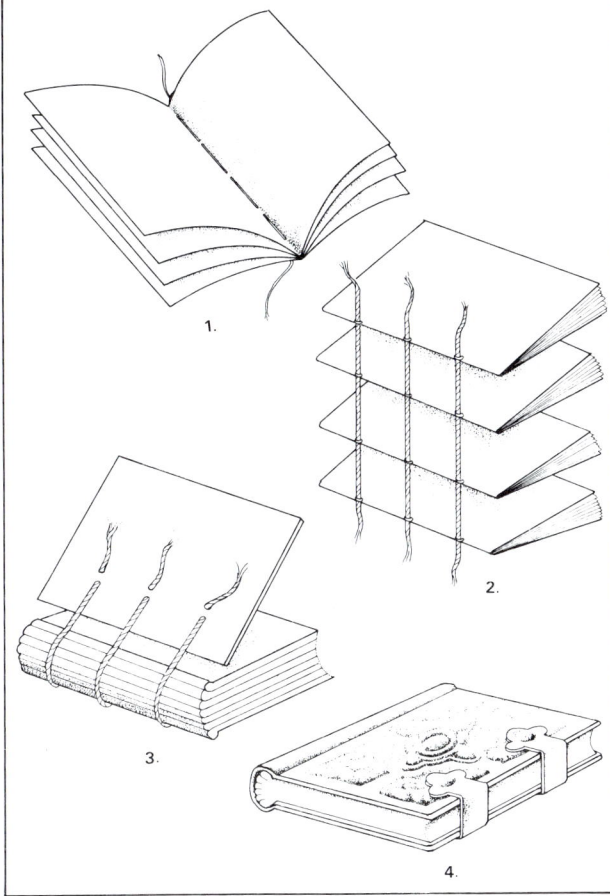

F 1. Folding a gathering of four pages and running a stitch up the middle.
2. Stitching the spines of the gathering together.
3. Binding and stitching the whole book between wooden covers, or boards.
4. The finished book, with its covers bound in leather with metal decorations.

This book is about one very special author — Gerald of Wales. Only a minority of all the manuscripts written down through the ages still exist today. Thousands were destroyed in wars, in fires or through the negligence of their owners. It is almost a miracle that a large number of books by a single author should have survived the hazards of the centuries. It is especially important to us in Wales that their author was a Welshman, and that much of his work describes Wales and its people. Many of the documents that remain from the Middle Ages are chronicles which list events, letters about official business, financial accounts or poetry. Gerald's work is different from all of these. Read these extracts from different documents G – I and judge what were the main differences between them and Gerald's work J

G 1164: And then the king, and the advanced forces along with him, encamped on the Berwyn mountains. And after he had stayed there a few days, he was oppressed by a mighty tempest of wind and exceeding torrents of rain. And when provisions had failed him, he withdrew his tents and his host [forces] to the open land of the flats of England.

('Brut y Tywysogyon', trans. Thomas Jones)

H John, by the grace of God. Be it known to you that we have given, and by this **charter** have confirmed, to the Lord Henry, Bishop of Llandaff and his successors, the holding of one fair annually at Llandaff to last for four days, namely the day after Whitsun and the three following days. And they may hold one market there each week on Sunday. Be it so in case the fair and market prove harmful to nearby fairs and markets.

(An old charter by King John to Llandaff, 1206)

I   TO RHIRID FLAIDD

There is a wolf who's glad to have me with him,
    A voice of his own raising;
Not a forest wolf, wild and wayward,
But a wolf of the field, courteous and kind.

A fame-flinging sword I wear on my hip
    Between shield and body;
A sword with a radiant blade;
Forceful Rhirid the Wolf's sword.

For Pennant's heir, pre-eminent a lord
    Among lords I compose,
Not a flock-stalking wolf I salute,
But a wolf for the bravest chieftains.

(A poem from about 1155-60 by Cynddelw Brydydd Mawr to Rhirid Flaidd (Rhirid the Wolf). He was the heir to Pennant Melangell in Powys. The poet praises a gift he has been given by Rhirid. What is that gift?)

J Only about three miles from Pembroke Castle is the fortified mansion known as Manorbier ... There the house stands, visible from afar because of its turrets and crenellations, on the top of a hill which is quite near the sea and which on the western side reaches as far as the harbour. To the north and north-west, just beneath the walls, there is an excellent fishpond ... On the same side there is a most attractive orchard, shut in between the fishpond and a grove of trees, with a great crag of rock and hazel-nut trees which grow to a great height ... Of all the different parts of Wales, Dyfed, with its seven cantrefs, is at once the most beautiful and the most productive. Of all Dyfed, the province of Pembroke is the most attractive; and in all Pembroke the spot which I have just described is most assuredly without its equal. It follows that in all the broad lands of Wales Manorbier is the most pleasant place by far.

(Gerald of Wales, *Itinerarium Kambriae*, trans. Lewis Thorpe)

Date	English Title	Latin Title
1188	The Conquest of Ireland	*Expugnatio Hibernica*
1188	The Topography of Ireland	*Topographia Hibernica*
1191	The Journey through Wales	*Itinerarium Kambriae*
1194	The Description of Wales	*Descriptio Kambriae*
1194	The Life of St David, Archbishop of Mynyw	*De Vita Sancti Davidis Menuensis Archiepiscopi*
1195	The Life of Godfrey, Archbishop of York	*De Vita Galfridi, Archiepiscopi Eboracensis*
1197	The Jewel of the Church	*Gemma Ecclesiastica*
1203	About his Deeds	*De Rebus a Se Gestis*
1216	About his Defamation	*De Invectionibus*
1216	The Mirror of Two Men	*Speculum Duorum*
1218	About the Authority and Status of the Church of Mynyw	*De Iure et Statu Menuensis Ecclesiae*

K

Table K lists the most important books by Gerald of Wales, their titles and their dates.

1. Imagine you are visiting a monastery in Gerald's time to ask about the books they are working on. Imagine a conversation between yourself and one of the monks.

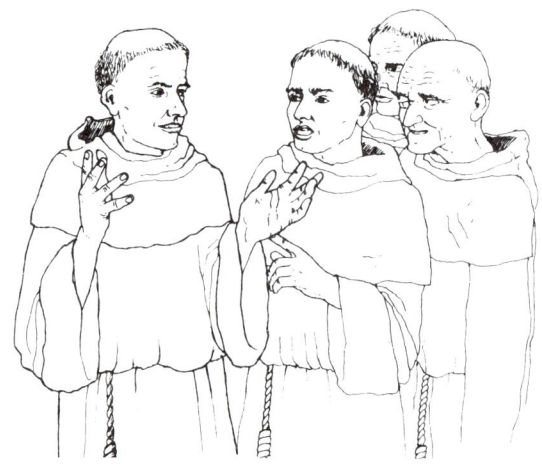

2. WALES IN GERALD'S TIME

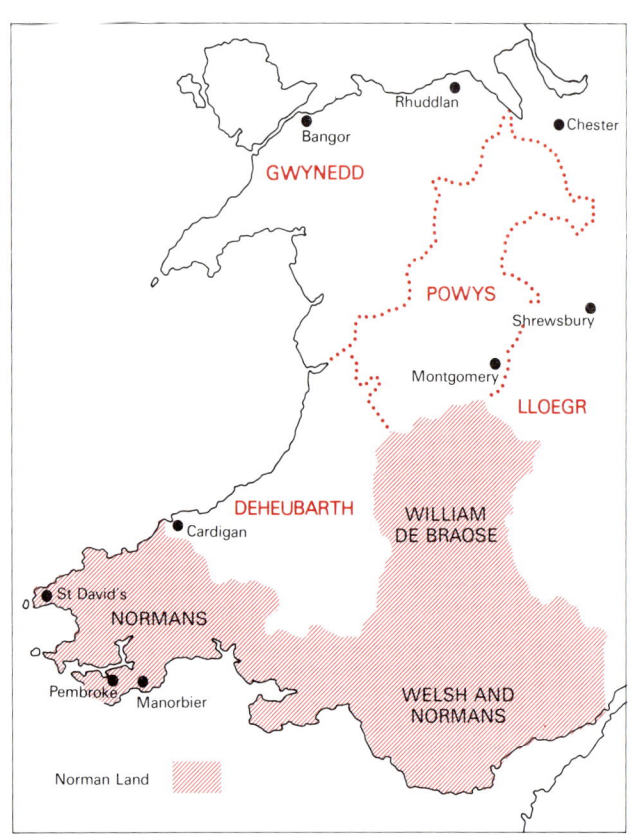

A Wales in Gerald's time.

Wales was a land facing conquest by a powerful enemy in 1146 — the year Gerald of Wales was born. A The Normans had carved out large slices of the country as lordships for themselves and had lived there for almost a century. Gerald himself was related to these Normans and to the Welsh who were fighting against them. During Gerald's long life the Welsh struck back strongly, the Normans reached out to invade Ireland and a series of kings struggled hard to keep a firm grip on all these happenings.

In this book we shall be looking at Gerald's background — the world he saw and lived in. We shall look at Wales and England, Ireland, Christian Europe and the Catholic Church, seeing them mainly through Gerald's eyes. It is against this background that we must look at Gerald's life. He stands amid the hurly-burly of his age, and we must look at that age as well as Gerald's own life-story if we are to understand him.

WALES — THE 'WILD WEST'

Wales was a lawless and violent **frontier** when Gerald of Wales was a boy. By that time Welsh and Norman lords were bordering each other, as in map A. The different lords eyed each other suspiciously, but often a Norman married a Welsh woman or a Welshman a Norman woman. Families of varied backgrounds, like that of Gerald, sprang up; we know that Gerald was proud of being related to both nations.

B

We should remember that Welsh and Norman lords were still fighting each other in Wales. Yet it was seldom a full-scale war and not a continuous one. Quarrels simply burst out into bloody fighting from time to time over a tract of land, involving the 'private armies' of rival families or even a member of the same family. Welsh lords had always tried to be independent of kings — Welsh ones or English ones — whenever they could. There wasn't a very strong feeling among the Welsh people of belonging to one country. Wales was divided into a patchwork of small units known as commotes and cantrefi, and a group of these units under one leader's control made up a lordship. Ancient custom gave each lord the right to rule like a king in his own territory. He had no real master. So a lord with one tiny commote under his control could claim just as much power over his own land as the prince of Deheubarth had over the dozens of commotes in his possession. B and C

1. Why do you think the Welsh lords were so unwilling to ally together? Explain in your own words what made cantrefi and commotes important in Medieval Wales.

Before the Normans came a strong king or prince in Wales might succeed for a time in conquering or controlling a large part of the country, but when he died the kingdom would collapse because each of his sons would claim a share of the father's lands. This resulted in princes' sons fighting each other, and Wales could never unite under a single king — except the king of England. After Henry II ascended to the English throne in 1154 no Welsh leader was supposed to call himself a king: they were princes or lords, and they had to pay homage, or swear loyalty, to the king of England.

C Two cantrefi in Deheubarth.

DANGER IN DYFED

Extract D describes a skirmish that took place in Dyfed in 1116, many years before Gerald was born. Indeed, Gerald's grandfather, Gerald de Windsor, had a lot to do with it, because Owain ap Cadwgan had kidnapped his wife Nest seven years before:

D In the meantime a host of the Flemings from Rhos chanced to come to Carmarthen to meet the king's son, and Gerald the steward along with them. Lo, those who had escaped coming with a cry towards the castle and making it known that they had been plundered and pillaged by Owain ap Cadwgan. And when the Flemings heard that, they were fired with hateful envy towards Owain because of the frequent injuries that Owain's comrades had previously inflicted upon them. And at the instigation of Gerald the steward, the man whose castle Owain had burned and whose wife Nest, together with his booty and spoils he had carried off by force, they pursued him. But Owain, not thinking that there was opposition to him, went on his way calmly. They, however, in pursuit of him quickly came to the place where he was, and the spoils with him. And when Owain's comrades saw a huge multitude pursuing them, they said to him, 'Behold a huge multitude pursuing us, with none able to resist them'. And he gave them answer, 'Be not afraid' said he, 'for they are the forces of the Flemings'. And having said that, he fell upon them in an attack. And they bore his attack manfully. After arrows had been shot on either side, Owain fell wounded. And after he had fallen, his comrades turned to flight ...

('Brut y Tywysogyon' trans. Thomas Jones)

2. What does this extract tell you about Wales in the twelfth century? What kind of country do you think it was to live in at that time?

Rhys ap Tewdwr, Gerald of Wales's grandfather, had been the last independent king of Deheubarth. He was killed in battle in 1093 and Dyfed was seized by the Norman family of Roger de Montgomery. It was his brother Arnulf who put Gerald de Windsor in charge of his castle at Pembroke. It was quite a sensible step therefore for Gerald to win some land for himself by marrying Nest, and taking over some of her father's land. Their own daughter, Angharad, later married another Norman knight E, William de Barri. This family owned land in Glamorgan already, including Barry Island. Gerald claimed that this was where they got their family name from. It was not at Barry, however, that William and Angharad settled to raise their own children, but on their new land in Pembrokeshire — at Manorbier.

E A Norman knight.

3. What strikes you as unusual about the relationship between Gerald's family on his mother's side and on his father's side? G

F Manorbier Castle near Pembroke, Gerald's childhood home.

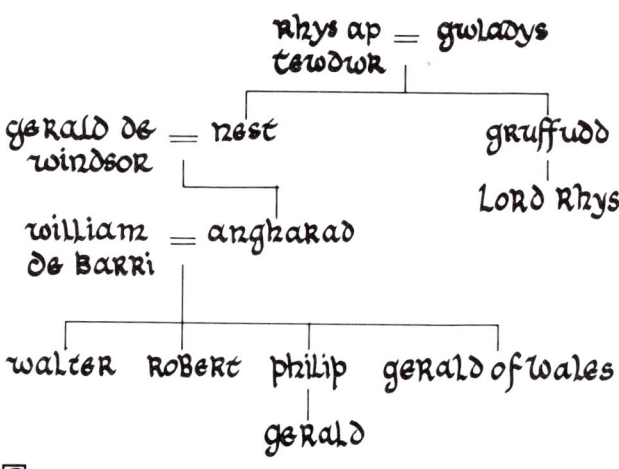

G Gerald's family tree.

3. THE INVASION OF IRELAND

A

By Gerald's time the Normans had missed their chance of conquering more land in Wales. Now it was the turn of the Welsh to be on the winning side. There were a number of strong princes among the Welsh — especially Owain Gwynedd and the Lord Rhys — and the Normans lost a great deal of land to them. So it was no surprise that some Normans looked to another land for fresh conquests and new territories. A

THE NORMANS IN IRELAND

There was a strong link between Gerald's family and Ireland. The de Barri family were proud of being related to the old Norman knights with their traditions of conquest and fighting. One of their ancestors had probably come from Normandy with the army of William the Conqueror when he seized the crown of England from the Saxon king Harold in 1066. One historian has written that it was a knight named Barri who gave his name to Glamorgan's Barry Island which is such a popular holiday centre today. Gerald however, thought that his family had adopted the name from the island.

One of Gerald's relatives was a man named Robert Fitz Stephen. He was another of the sons of Nest, a strong warrior who longed to conquer more land for himself and his family. Ireland, at this time was completely independent of England, just like Scotland. Some parts of Wales were free in day-to-day matters too, but the closeness of England meant that Welsh independence was more fragile than that of Ireland and Scotland.

In 1166 Dermot, king of Leinster in Ireland asked King Henry II to help him regain his kingdom after he had been overthrown by his enemies. Henry was too busy, but he suggested to Dermot that some of the Norman lords in Wales might be ready to help him.

And so it was. Dermot and Robert Fitz Stephen made an agreement that Robert and his relatives would help Dermot to regain his kingdom on condition that they were given land for themselves in Ireland. In 1169 a force of some 300-400 men, about 40 of them imported knights, sailed to Ireland, and on May Day they landed at Bannow Bay in the south of the modern county of Wexford.

1. Why did the Normans from Wales invade Ireland in 1169?

At first the campaign was a success. The stronghold of Wexford and the Ossory districts were overrun, but then other tribes in Ireland rose up against them and the fighting grew harder. Richard de Clare, who was called Strongbow, came to Ireland in 1170. He was the son of another Norman lord who had conquered large areas of Wales for himself. Henry II had hinted that Strongbow might go there to join the conquest. He landed on 23 August 1170, with 200 knights and 1,000 foot soldiers, or infantry. He and the sons of Nest captured Waterford and Dublin, and restored Dermot to his old kingdoms. Dermot had promised his daughter in marriage to Strongbow in return for his help. After the victory the marriage took place, and Dermot himself died not long afterwards. Richard de Clare, Earl of Pembroke and Strigul, now became King of Leinster.

HENRY II IN IRELAND

The news from Ireland came as a shock to Henry. He did not want to see his own lords, including Strongbow becoming independent kings in Ireland. That is exactly what had happened in Sicily after a group of Normans arrived there many years before. They made the island into a completely independent kingdom. Henry decided that the only way to prevent such a thing happening was to lead the conquest himself.

In 1171-72 Henry came with an army to Pembroke, and sailed from there to Ireland to show who was master. Once there he made sure that the Normans in Ireland paid **homage** to him, and accepted his authority over them. These Norman families, the Geraldines and the Clares in particular, played an important part in the history of the island for centuries after.

2. Imagine you are a priest sent by the Pope to see what was happening in Ireland. Prepare a report about what had happened there up to the end of Henry II's visit in 1172.

GERALD'S RELATIONS IN IRELAND

Several members of Gerald's family fought in Ireland. Robert Fitz Stephen was Gerald's half-uncle, and over the centuries Irish historians have called the whole campaign of 1169 and after 'the conquest of the sons of Nest'. Another name often given to these conquerors was 'the Geraldines', although they weren't all members of the Fitzgerald family, or sons of Nest for that matter. But the names show how important Gerald's relations were in the history of Ireland at that time.

Gerald himself first went to Ireland with his brother Philip in 1183. He did not stay long on that occasion; in 1185 he returned in the company of Prince John, Henry II's younger son.

Gerald never praised the Irish much but he was often critical of the Welsh too, as we shall see. Extract B is a description which Gerald had probably heard from someone else of a king-making ceremony, in Donegal. Irish historians insisted for years that the story was completely false.

B When the whole people of that land has been gathered together in one place, a white mare is brought forward into the middle of the assembly. He who is to be inaugurated, comes forward on all fours not as a chief, but as a beast, not as a king, but as an **outlaw** ... professing himself to be a beast also. The mare is then killed immediately, cut up in pieces, and boiled in water. A bath is prepared for the man afterwards in the same water. He sits in the bath surrounded by all his people, and all, he and they, eat of the meat of the mare which is brought to them. He quaffs and drinks of the broth in which he is bathed, not in any cup, or using his hand, but just dipping his mouth into it round about him. When this unrighteous rite has been carried out, his kingship and dominion have been confirmed.

(Gerald of Wales, *Topographia Hibernica* trans. John J. O'Mears)

3. What do you think Gerald's opinion of this custom was? What does the extract reveal about Gerald's attitude towards the Irish?

C An Irish king-making ceremony.

The book *Expugnatio Hibernica* is largely the story of Gerald's own relations, as well as the story of Henry II's part in the campaign. He writes of the king's other troubles as well: including the story of the murder of Thomas à Becket, Archbishop of Canterbury, by four of the king's knights in 1170. As he writes about his own family his Norman pride shows clearly: D

D Who thrust into the heart of the enemy's territory? The Geraldines. Who kept them in obedience? The Geraldines. Who arouses the greatest fear among the enemy? The Geraldines. Against whom are the blows of malice principally aimed? The Geraldines. Oh, that they had not found a prince who would have made the most of their worth and fame! How quiet, how peaceful the condition of Ireland would have been under their rule. But they were kept under groundless suspicion while others, with none of their virtues, were trusted.

(Gerald of Wales *Expugnatio Hibernica*)

4. In what words above did Gerald claim that unfair accusations were being made against members of his family.
5. Name the following:
   a) the bay where the Normans first landed;
   b) the King of Leinster who was in exile in 1166;
   c) the other name given to the Sons of Nest;
   d) the nickname given to Richard de Clare;
   e) the relative of Gerald's who played a leading part in the invasion of Ireland.

4. GERALD AND THE CROWN

The person mentioned most often in Gerald's books is Henry II, king of England from 1154-1189. 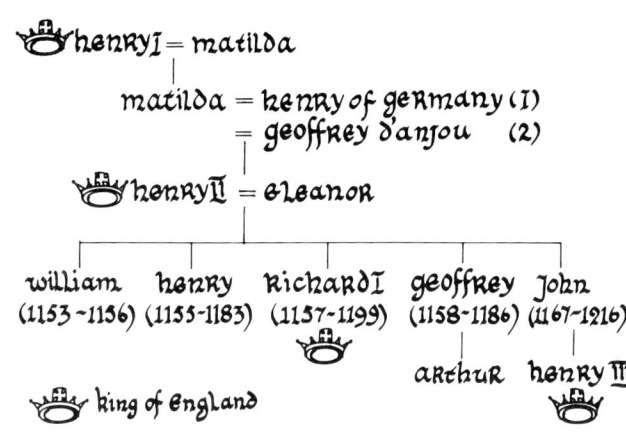 Gerald worked for him for a time. You will see in this chapter the strength and determination that made him such a powerful king. Yet he was unhappy in his relations with his own sons. The genealogical table B shows the royal family in the twelfth century. Gerald's grandfather had been an officer of king Henry I, and Gerald himself served Henry II, Richard II, and John.

A Henry II (1154-89).

HENRY II AND HIS FAMILY

Henry became king in 1154, after struggling for years to gain the crown. He performed a remarkable feat in getting his kingdom under firm control. Although he was related to the Norman royal family, his roots lay deeper in France than in England. After

B Henry II's family tree.

the death of William the Conqueror in 1087 two of his sons had become kings in turn — William Rufus (1087-1100) and Henry I (1100-35).

After Henry I's death his daughter Matilda should have inherited the throne.  But a cousin of hers, Stephen of Blois, seized the throne and a civil war raged between the supporters of both sides for years. Although Matilda won a brief victory in 1141, she soon lost control after a revolt in London and the fighting started up again.

C Queen Matilda's seal.

Matilda had married a warlike lord of France — Geoffrey of Anjou, and he gave her powerful support in her struggle against Stephen. After Geoffrey's sudden death in the prime of life, their son, Henry, took up the struggle. Henry led a new campaign to England in 1151 and by 1153 he had forced the ageing king Stephen to agree that Henry should inherit the throne after Stephen's death. After

Stephen died in 1154 Henry became king of England. His wife Eleanor was mistress of the large, rich duchy of Aquitaine. Map D shows the vast territory over which Henry was now king — the whole of England, most of Wales and most of France too.

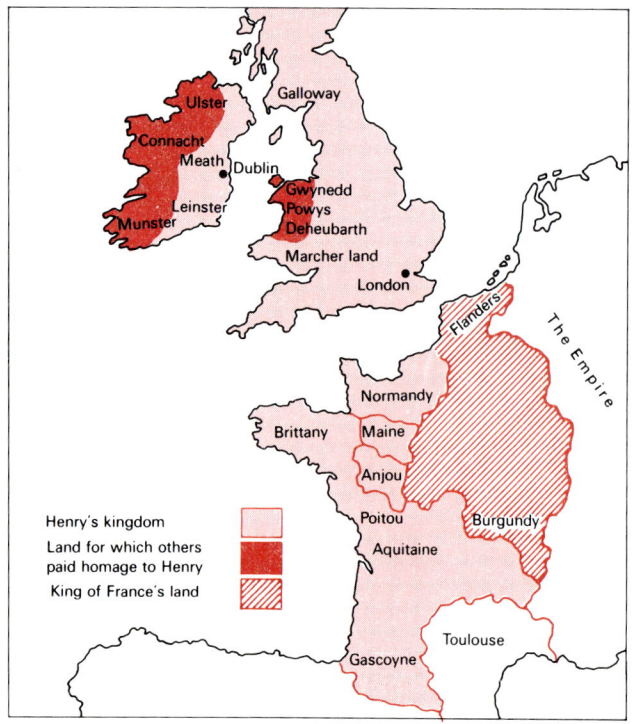

D Henry II's territories.

The sheer size of the territories was the main cause of Henry's troubles. The king of France claimed that Henry should pay homage to him for all his lands in France, and there were other disputes between them over lands which they both claimed. Henry fought against the French king Louis VIII and his son Philip II for most of his life. King Philip II won such respect among the French people that they called him Philip Augustus (Philip the Great). Philip was especially keen to regain the land France had lost to Henry II and his family.

Quite apart from these problems, Henry also went to war twice in Wales — against Owain Gwynedd, in 1157 and 1164. He struck deep into Snowdonia but he suffered heavy losses, and was almost killed in a surprise attack by Owain's men. The 1157 campaign ended with a peace treaty between Henry and Owain. In 1164 Henry brought a larger army, but other princes, including the Lord Rhys, united with Owain to resist the English. Bad weather also hindered Henry's advance, and he had to withdraw. Photo E shows a tomb which is said to be that of Owain Gwynedd.

By all accounts Henry was a very hard-working and energetic man. This is what Gerald wrote about him: F

F Henry II, king of England, had a red face, rather dark with a great round head. His eyes were grey, and they flashed when he was angry. He presented a fiery appearance, his voice trembled and his neck was rather hunched; but he had a broad chest and muscular arms. His body was thickset and he had a great belly, more by an accident of nature than by overeating. For he ate moderately, and indeed was temperate in everything, miserly even, considering that he was a prince ... In time of war he took only a little rest, even in the intervals between business and battle. Times of peace were not seasons of laziness and ease for him, because he was overfond of hunting and devoted himself to it with gusto. At the first glimmer of dawn he would mount a fast horse and spend the day riding tirelessly through the woods, penetrating the depths of the forest and crossing over the crests of the hills. After returning home in the evening, he was seldom to be seen sitting down, either before or after supper, because in spite of his great tiredness he would exhaust the whole court by remaining constantly on his feet ... He could be numbered among the men of medium height, unlike his sons; the eldest two were taller than the average and the younger two shorter.

(Gerald of Wales, *Expugnatio Hibernica*)

1. Study picture A and extract F and make a head-to-toe portrait of Henry as you imagine he looked.

E The supposed tomb of Owain Gwynedd in Bangor Cathedral.

Gerald may have been at the king's court when Henry II died in France in 1189. The king's relationship with his sons had been very bitter during his last years. His eldest son had rebelled against him in 1173, with the support of the French, the Scots and the English barons. Henry defeated them all. Later on the same son (also called Henry) went to war against his younger brother Richard, who was ruling Aquitaine on his father's behalf. Two sons died soon after — Henry and Geoffrey — but Richard then started to demand more freedom for himself and he fought twice against his father, in 1185 and 1189.

On the last occasion Richard struck a bargain with his father's old enemy, Philip Augustus, king of France. G It was a cruel blow for Henry when his younger son, John, joined in this rebellion.

G

Henry was at his old home, Chinon in Anjou when he died on 7 July, 1189. Here is a description of the king's last days, based on the account Gerald wrote in one of his last books, *De Instructione Principis*, ('How to educate a prince'): H

H The Old King was dying, of the illness which had afflicted him all that summer; but what actually killed him was the knowledge that John had joined his foes. All his troubles had come upon him, and he knew it, because he had schemed to give John the rightful inheritance of his brothers. When he had glanced at the list, headed by John's name, he exclaimed in anguish: 'Can it be true that my darling John has forsaken me? He whom I loved beyond my other sons, and for whose advancement I have brought upon me all these evils?'

He was lying on his bed, though still fully dressed. Now he turned his face to the wall and cried: 'Let things go as they will. I shall struggle no longer. He did not speak again, and on the same day he died.

(Alfred Duggan, *Devil's Brood*)

2. What do you think is happening in picture I?

I

Gerald saw the troubles Henry suffered as a punishment from God for offending the Church. He especially recalled the murder of Thomas à Becket in 1170. In Cardiff in 1172, as Henry was returning home from Ireland, an old man prophesized that he would suffer some great wrong at the hands of those he loved most if he did not improve his attitude towards the Church. Within a year his eldest son had launched his first rebellion.

3. By doing your own research gather details of the life and reign of Henry II and make notes of the facts you discover.

4. Why was Henry so often at war during his reign?

THE CRUSADES

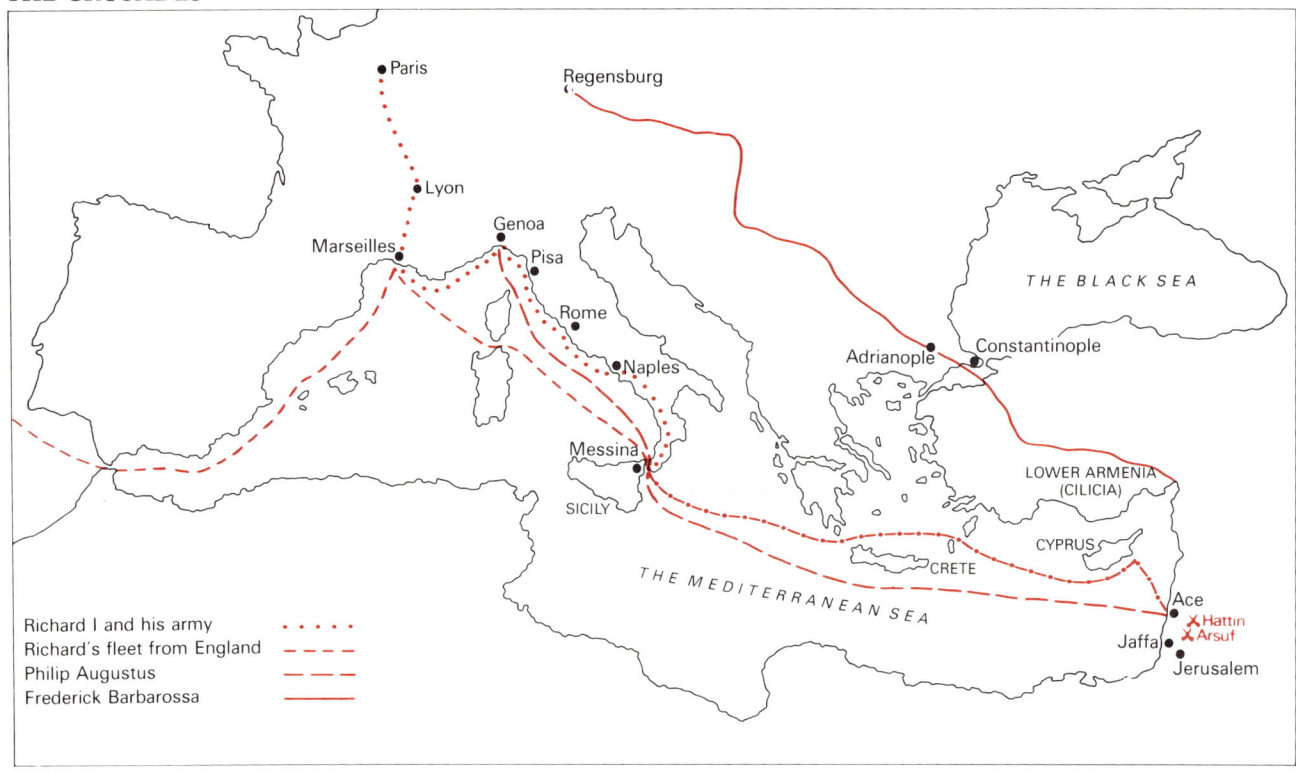

J A map of Europe during the third crusade.

Look at map J. It shows where the crusade was in Gerald's time.

The Crusades were a series of wars aimed at capturing Palestine, the ancient land of Jesus Christ and the Bible, from the Turks. Ever since the seventh century, when a young Arab prince called Muhammad had a vision which made him the prophet of a new religion, the Middle East had been a cauldron of war. By AD 800 Muhammad's followers had conquered much of the Middle East in the name of their religion, Islam.

Seeing the Bible lands — especially Bethlehem, Nazareth and Jerusalem being ruled by people of a different religion was painful for many in Europe. Christians had regained Palestine in the tenth century, but a century later a new tribe of fierce warriors turned the tables again. These were the Turks. They conquered most of the Arab lands and the Turks themselves adopted the Islamic religion. In 1071 the Turks conquered Palestine. It became more difficult for pilgrims to visit the Holy land because of Turkish hostility. An urge developed in Europe to **liberate** the Bible lands from the infidel, as those who were not Christians were called.

Jerusalem had many sites that were important to Christians. The most sacred was the Church of the Holy Sepulchre, built by the Emperor Constantine over the spot where Jesus Christ was believed to have been buried. A chapel also stood above the place where Jesus had been crucified. Many of the pilgrims who came there believed they also knew where the Garden of Gethsemane was, the place where Jesus had prayed before he was arrested by the guards. People felt that no sacrifice was too great to protect these sites.

5.   What was the aim of the Crusades?

In 1095 Pope Urban II K called for a Crusade to free Jerusalem from the Turks, and thousands flocked to take the Cross — to wear the sign of Christ's cross

K Pope Urban II.

over their armour. The first Crusade (1096-99) was a success. Jerusalem was captured and an independent kingdom was set up there under the leadership of one of the heroes of the war. Half a century later, after the Turks had massacred all the Christians in the city of Edessa there was a second Crusade (1147-49), but it was not so successful. Then in 1187 the remainder of the kingdom of Jerusalem fell into Turkish hands again. The call for a third Crusade went up all over Europe.

Gerald accompanied Baldwin, Archbishop of Canterbury, on a famous journey through Wales in 1188. Its aim was to persuade Welshmen to join in the third Crusade. In about five weeks some 3,000 men promised to serve in the Crusader armies. Gerald used the things he had seen and heard on this journey, together with his wide knowledge of Wales since childhood, to write two books, *Itinerarium Kambriae* ('The Journey through Wales') and *Descripto Kambriae* ('Description of Wales').

Richard I, Henry II's warrior son, succeeded his father on the throne of England. [L] He spent nearly the whole of his reign out of England. He went on the Crusade to Palestine in 1190. He became famous during the attack on the city of Acre, fighting alongside his father's old enemy, Philip Augustus. The city was captured, and Saladin, the Turkish king, held Richard in great respect. In 1192 Richard made a favourable peace treaty with Saladin.

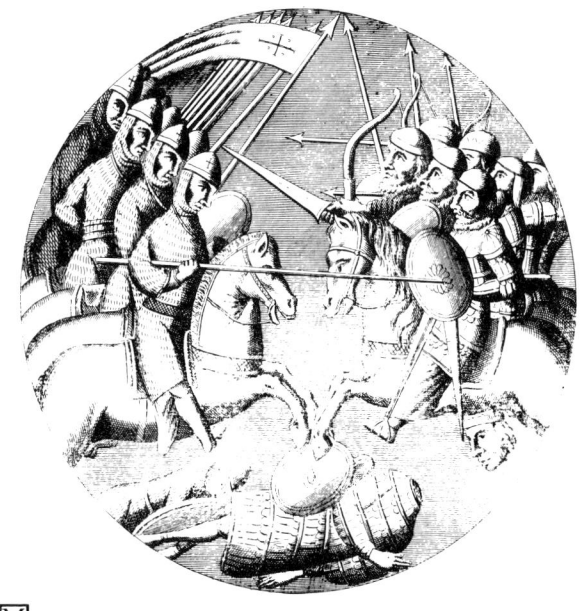

[M]

Picture [M] shows a Crusader army fighting the Turks. But there were few head-on battles like this in the Crusades. One of the favourite tactics of the Turks was the surprise ambush — the very tactic the Welsh adopted in Gwynedd. The Crusaders had to spend months at a time besieging strong fortress cities such as Antioch, Acre and Jerusalem.

[L] Richard I (1189-99).

Picture N shows the massive attack that won control of Jerusalem in 1099.

N

6. Look carefully at picture N. What else, other than the attack, is happening in it? Why is this scene shown in the picture?

In picture O a Crusader can be seen kneeling in prayer. People in the Middle Ages liked to believe that the Crusaders were fighting for a religious purpose. But many of them went to war, for the rich plunder that could be won, or simply for adventure.

7. What is the Crusader wearing in picture O? What disadvantage did dressing like this in the Middle East cause?

8. Imagine you are on the Crusade with Richard I. Write about your adventures.

On his way home from the Crusade in 1193, Richard was kidnapped and held hostage by an old enemy of his, the Archduke of Austria. Picture P shows Richard, dressed as a poor pilgrim, being captured by the Austrians. The king was imprisoned for months on end, and none of his people knew where he was. Then, according to an old popular tale, his court minstrel Blondel had been wandering all over Europe in search of his king, and as he rested in the shadow of a castle wall in Germany he sang one verse of a song. Imagine his surprise when another voice sang the second verse — a song only he and king Richard knew!

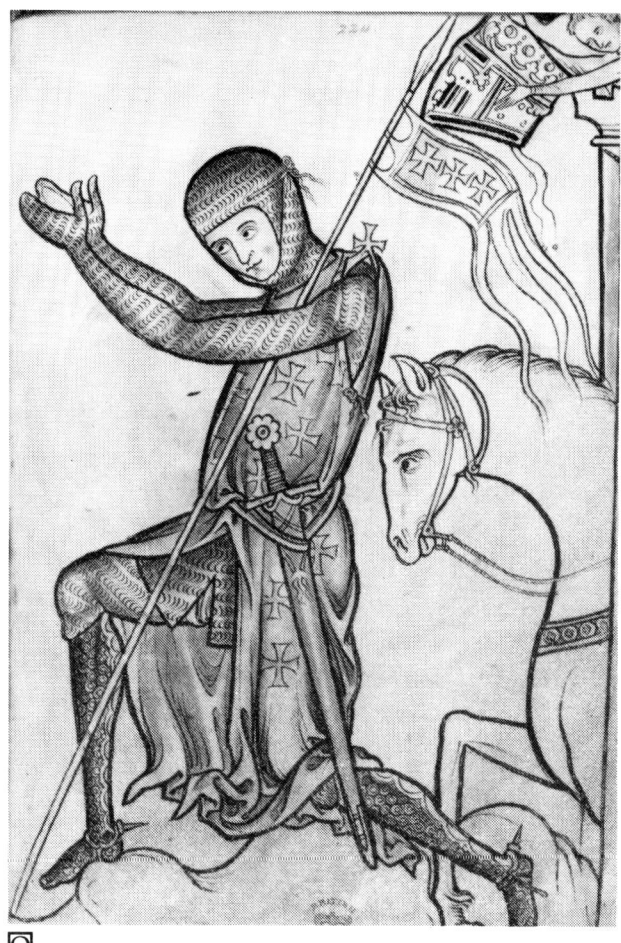

O

P A picture from a manuscript of the time showing Richard being captured. Why do you think the king was dressed like this?

Whether the story of Blondel is true or not, the news about Richard reached England. Richard's mother, Queen Eleanor, raised the huge ransom that was demanded for his return, and in 1194 Richard returned to England. He stayed for only some three months, however, before going to fight in France —

16

back to the old struggle over his family's territories. Richard died in France in April 1199. He was killed by an arrow while besieging a fortified town in a French lordship.

9. What kind of man was Richard in your opinion? Does the name 'Coeur de Lion' (lion-heart) which was used to describe him suggest anything to you?

10. Which of the following, in your opinion, was the most interesting character and why? (a) Owain Gwynedd, (b) Stephen of Blois, (c) Richard I, (d) Phillip Augustus.

11. Imagine that you are a priest trying to entice people to join the Crusade: explain to your audience (your class) what had happened in the Middle East up to 1187, and why they should join the Crusade.

5. GERALD'S VIEW OF WALES

A A portrait of Gerald from an old manuscript.

When he wrote about Wales, Gerald not only told the story of his journey with Archbishop Baldwin, but he also described the land and its people in detail. Not many full accounts of what individual countries were like in medieval times have survived. But Gerald did more than simply describe: he sometimes expressed his own opinion about both the Welsh and the Normans. He himself, of course, belonged to both nations.

GERALD'S BOOK

'The Journey through Wales' is a wonderful book. It describes interesting places and important people in all parts of Wales, and retells stories and legends about the places Gerald visited. The land, the people's customs and the personalities of men like the Lord Rhys and Owain Cyfeiliog come to life in its pages. He also describes Welsh bishops, Norman lords and, of course, Henry II and Archbishop Baldwin — the two men who were mainly responsible for the journey. This is how Gerald described Baldwin: **B**

B He was a swarthy man, with an honest, venerable face, only moderately tall, of good physique and inclined to be thin rather than corpulent. He was modest and sober, and of great abstinence and self-control, so that very little criticism was ever levelled against him ...

(Gerald of Wales, *Itinerarium Kambriae*, trans. Lewis Thorpe)

At an early stage in that journey, long ago in 1188, the party visited Llan-ddew, where Gerald's official home was as **Archdeacon** of Brecknock. They were travelling through his district now: **C**

C This region produces a great amount of corn. If there is ever a shortage, supplies are quickly brought in from the neighbouring parts of England. There is ample pasture and plenty of woodland, the first full of cattle, the second teeming with wild animals. There is no lack of freshwater fish, both in the Usk and the Wye. Salmon and trout are fished from these rivers, but the Wye has more salmon and the Usk more trout.

(Gerald of Wales, *Itinerarium Kambriae*, trans. Lewis Thorpe)

The book gives many examples to show how violent Wales was in the twelfth century. Here is one incident that Gerald saw as the party travelled through South Wales. They were heading westwards now, and approaching the Cistercian abbey of Whitland, an abbey said to have been founded by St David himself. Baldwin himself was a Cistercian monk: **D**

D When we were travelling from Carmarthen to the Cistercian monastery called Whitland, the Archbishop was told by messengers of how a young Welshman, who was coming to meet him in all devotion, had been murdered on the way by his enemies. He turned aside from the road, ordered the bloody corpse to be wrapped up in his almoner's cloak, and with pious supplication prayer commended the soul of the murdered youth to heaven. The next day twelve archers from the near-by castle of St Clears, who had killed the young man, were signed with the Cross in Whitland as a punishment for their crime.

(Gerald of Wales, *Itinerarium Kambriae*, trans. Lewis Thorpe)

E Snowdonia and the summit of Snowdon.

1. Do you know of any important events in Welsh history, before Gerald's time, which are said to have taken place at Whitland?

In another chapter Gerald gives a dramatic description of the mountains of Snowdonia. E Gwynedd was able to remain independent for so long because Snowdonia made it a natural fortress. F

F I must not fail to tell you about the mountains which are called Eryri by the Welsh and by the English Snowdonia, that is the Snow Mountains. They rise gradually from the land of the sons of Cynan and extend northwards near Degannwy. When looked at from Anglesey, they seem to rear their lofty summits right up to the clouds. They are thought to be so enormous and to extend so far that, as the old saying goes: 'just as Anglesey can supply all the inhabitants of Wales with corn, so, if all the herds were gathered together, Snowdonia could afford sufficient pasture.

(Gerald of Wales, *Itinerarium Kambriae*, trans. Lewis Thorpe)

GERALD AND WALES

Gerald sometimes mentions the Welsh language in his books. He clearly understood the language well, but how well do you think he spoke it, judging by extracts G and H?

G In Usk Castle a large group of men was signed with the Cross. This was the result of the Archbishop's sermon and of an address by that good and honest man, William, Bishop of Llandaff, who remained constantly at our side as long as we were in his **diocese**. Alexander, Archdeacon of Bangor, acted as interpreter for the Welsh.

(Gerald of Wales, *Itinerarium Kambriae*, trans. Lewis Thorpe)

H In Haverfordwest first the Archbishop gave a sermon, and then the word of God was preached with some eloquence by the Archdeacon of St David's, the man whose name appears on the title page of this book, in short by me. A great crowd of people assembled, some of them soldiers, others civilians. Many found it odd and some, indeed, thought it little short of miraculous, that when I, the Archdeacon, preached the word of God, speaking first in Latin and then in French, those who could not understand a word of either language were just as much moved to tears as the others, rushing forward in equal numbers to receive the sign of the Cross.

(Gerald of Wales, *Itinerarium Kambriae*, trans. Lewis Thorpe)

The Lord Rhys's court jester once made this comment after Gerald had been preaching to win recruits for the Crusade: **I**

I 'O Rhys, you ought greatly to love this kinsman of yours, the Archdeacon; for today he has sent a hundred of your men or more to serve Christ; and if he had spoken in Welsh, I do not think that a single man would have been left you out of all this multitude.'

(Gerald of Wales, *De Rebus a Se Gestis*, trans H. E. Butler)

2. Judging from extract **I**, how good a speaker would you say Gerald was whatever language he spoke?

This is what Gerald had to say about the Welsh language: **J** and **K**.

J It is thought that the Welsh language is richer, more carefully pronounced and preferable in all respects in North Wales, for that area has far fewer foreigners. Others maintain that the speech of Cardiganshire in South Wales is better articulated and more to be admired, since it is in the middle and the heartland of Wales. In both Cornwall and Brittany they speak almost the same language as in Wales. It comes from the same root and is intelligible to the Welsh in many instances, and almost in all. It is rougher and less clearly pronounced, but probably closer to the original British speech, or so I think myself.

(Gerald of Wales, *Descriptio Kambriae*, trans. Lewis Thorpe)

K In their narrative poems and declamations they are so inventive and ingenious that, when using their native tongue, they produce works of art which are at once attractive and highly original, both in the choice of words and the sentiments expressed. You will find many poets in Wales, bards, as they call them, who devote their energies to this kind of composition:
   'Stern bards who many an austere epic song
   have sung.'
More than any other rhetorical figure they delight in alliteration, and especially that which links together the initial letters or syllables of words ...

'*Dichon Duw da i unig*'
'*Erbyn di-bwyll pwyll parod*'

(Gerald of Wales, *Descriptio Kambriae*, trans. Lewis Thorpe)

3. Find out what the modern Welsh name is for a pattern of 'hard' letters, or consonants, answering each other in poetry.

4. What difference did Gerald detect between the ways Welsh was spoken in different parts of Wales?

To what extent was Gerald really Welsh? Gerald's Wales included the Norman lands too, but to him the Welsh people were those who spoke Welsh and had lived according to the old customs of the country. Although Llywelyn ap Iorwerth and Madog of Powys had supported him in his campaign over St David's, Gerald had a poor opinion of the Welsh people. This can be seen in the book *Descriptio Kambriae* ('Description of Wales') in 1194. The book is divided into two parts. In the first Gerald listed the good features of the Welsh as well as describing the Welsh landscape. In the second part he wrote about the bad features of the Welsh, as well as the best way to conquer Wales, and the best way the Welsh might fight back. The book started with the geography of Wales: **L**

L Cambria is called Wales nowadays, that having become its usual name, although it is a foreign word and not really correct. It is two hundred miles long and about one hundred miles wide. It takes some eight days to travel the whole length, from the mouth of the River Gwygir in Anglesey to Portskewett in Gwent. In breadth it stretches from Porth-mawr, that is the Great Port, near St David's, to Rhyd-helyg, the Welsh for Willow Ford, called Walford in English, this being a journey which lasts four days. Because of its high mountains, deep valleys and extensive forests, not to mention its rivers and marshes, it is not easy of access.

(Gerald of Wales, *Descriptio Kambriae*, trans. Lewis Thorpe)

5. How long did it take in Gerald's time to travel from south to north Wales?

the court ... They plough the soil once in March and April for oats, a second time in summer, and then they turn it a third time while the grain is being threshed. In this way the whole population lives almost entirely on oats and the produce of their herds, milk, cheese and butter. They eat plenty of meat, but little bread. They pay no attention to commerce, shipping or industry, and their only preoccupation is military training. They are passionately devoted to their freedom and to the defence of their country: for these they fight, for these they suffer hardships, for these they will take up their weapons and willingly sacrifice their lives.

(Gerald of Wales, *Descriptio Kambriae*, trans. Lewis Thorpe)

Picture O shows a Welsh archer.

O A Welsh archer.

M

6. Here is a very early map showing the whole of Wales. M It was drawn by Mathew Paris, who died in 1259. Can you recognize any part of Wales on the map? Do you think a map by Gerald himself might have been more accurate?

Gerald wrote once that he had drawn a map of Wales, showing its mountains, forests and its rivers. Perhaps this explains why most of his description was so accurate. After describing the land Gerald went on to describe the people, their characters and their customs. He concentrated first on the good points: N

N The Welsh people are light and agile. They are fierce rather than strong, and totally dedicated to the practice of arms. Not only the leaders but the entire nation are trained in war. Sound the trumpet for battle and the peasant will rush from his plough to pick up his weapons as quickly as the courtier from

Extract P gives a vivid description of a Welsh feast:

P You must not expect a variety of dishes from a Welsh kitchen, and there are no highly seasoned **confections** to whet your appetite. In a Welsh house there are no tables, no tablecloths and no napkins. Everyone behaves quite naturally, with no attempt whatsoever at etiquette [good manners]. You sit down in threes, not in pairs as elsewhere, and they put the food in front of you, all together, on a single large trencher [wooden plate] containing enough for three, resting on rushes and green grass. Sometimes they serve the main dish on bread, rolled out large and thin, and baked fresh each day ... Finally the time comes to retire to rest. Alongside one of the walls is placed a communal bed, stuffed with rushes, and not all that many of them ...

(Gerald of Wales, *Descriptio Kambriae*, trans. Lewis Thorpe)

Q A Welsh house from medieval Glamorgan.

Two of the leading officials of a Welsh court are shown in pictures R and T.

R A Welsh judge. What is he holding in his left hand?

Gerald wrote that a family's genealogy was important to the Welsh: S

S The Welsh value distinguished birth and noble descent more than anything else in the world ... Even the common people know their family-tree by heart and can readily recite from memory the list of their grandfathers, great-grandfathers, great-great-grandfathers, back to the sixth or seventh generation ... As they have this intense interest in their family descent, they avenge with great ferocity any wrong or insult done to their relations. They are vindictive by nature, bloodthirsty and violent. Not only are they ready to avenge new and recent injuries, but old ones, too, as if they had just received them.

(Gerald of Wales, *Descriptio Kambriae*, trans. Lewis Thorpe)

This section, remember, is the one where Gerald describes the good things about the Welsh! When he starts to list their faults he writes that they cannot

T A Welsh court falconer.

keep promises or treaties, and that they tell lies a lot of the time! Here is his account of how they behave in war: U

U In war the Welsh are very ferocious when battle is first joined ... From their first fierce and headlong onslaught attack, and the shower of javelins which they hurl, they seem most formidable opponents. If the enemy resists manfully and they are repulsed, they are immediately thrown into confusion. With further resistance they turn their backs, making no attempt at a counter-attack, but seeking safety in flight ... Although beaten today and shamefully put to flight with much slaughter, tomorrow they march out again, no whit dejected by their defeat or their losses. They may not shine in open combat and in fixed formation, but they harass the enemy by their ambushes and night-attacks. In a single battle they are easily beaten, but they are difficult to conquer in a long war.

(Gerald of Wales, *Descriptio Kambriae*, trans. Lewis Thorpe)

7. Why, in Gerald's view, was Wales a difficult country to conquer?

Gerald complained that the Welsh were quarrelsome people, always fighting or taking legal action against each other — even between members of the same family. These criticisms were followed by two sections that seemed completely opposed to one another. In the first he advised the Normans how best to defeat the Welsh and conquer them, and then he advised the Welsh how to resist. In his own

V A Welsh foot soldier.

words: 'I have set out the case for the English with considerable care and in some detail. I myself am descended from both peoples, and it seems only fair that I should now put the opposite point of view.' These are the tactics to defeat the Welsh: W

W He [the king] can never hope to conquer in one single battle a people which will never draw up its forces to engage an enemy army in the field, and will never allow itself to be besieged inside fortified strong-points ... he must sow dissension [disagreement] in their ranks and do all he can by promises and bribes to stir them up against each other. In the autumn not only the marches but certain carefully chosen localities in the interior must be fortified with castles, and these he must supply with ample provisions and garrison with families favourable to his cause.

(Gerald of Wales, *Descriptio Kambriae*, trans. Lewis Thorpe)

After defeating the Welsh, wrote Gerald, the king should appoint a determined, wise and fair-minded man to rule the country, to make sure that the laws were kept and that the Welsh themselves were fairly treated. In the first version that he wrote of this book, however, Gerald gave the English one piece of advice that is shockingly extreme. Indeed, it was very similar to what the Nazis tried to do in eastern Europe during the Second World War — uprooting the entire Welsh population, forcing them to leave the country and bringing in English settlers to replace them. Such a suggestion really makes it difficult to regard Gerald as Welsh at all. If a fair system of government failed, he wrote, the people should all be sent out of the country and resettled somewhere else: 'Indeed, it may well be thought preferable to eject the entire population which lives there now, so that Wales can be colonized anew. The present inhabitants are virtually ungovernable, and there are some who think that it would be 'far safer and more sensible to turn this rough and impenetrable country into an unpopulated forest area and game preserve.' In the second edition, however, he cut out this section. Gerald makes one vital point in his advice to the Welsh: they must learn to unite under one leader and stop fighting amongst themselves. If they did this, their chances would be improved. 'The English', said Gerald, 'are striving for power, the Welsh for freedom; the English are fighting for material gain, the Welsh to avoid a disaster; the English soldiers are hired mercenaries, the Welsh are defending their homeland.'

8. Write a story in your own words, describing Welsh everyday life as it is shown in extracts on p.21. Write as if you too were a visiting traveller, like Gerald.

9. Draw up a two-column table of things Gerald liked about the Welsh and the things he disliked.

6. GERALD AND HIS CHURCH

Gerald had wanted to be a priest ever since he was a child. His father, with an eye to the future, supported that wish.

CHOOSING A CAREER

In those days a father of a large and important family tried to make sure some sort of living had been arranged for all his children before they grew up. Usually the eldest son would inherit all or most of the estate; and a Norman father would try to arrange marriages with rich landowners for his daughters. His younger sons would cause him the most problems when it came to providing for them. He could not give them a large share of his property or the estate the eldest son inherited would be that much poorer. On the other hand, he had to do something for the younger sons. One way of finding a job for a younger son was through the Church. That is what happened in two generations of Gerald's family. One of his mother's brothers, David Fitzgerald, was Bishop of St David's from 1148 to 1176. Gerald's parents probably arranged for David to take charge of their younger son's education and to help him begin a career in the Church.

Gerald received a good education, and after returning from Paris at the age of 28 he carried out a number of tasks for the Church. In 1175 he was appointed Archdeacon of Brecknock. An Archdeacon was next in importance to a Bishop, and all the churches in a wide area would be under his control.

1. Why do you think it would have been dangerous for a lord not to arrange some kind of living for his younger sons?

THE PARISHES — TREE AND BRANCHES

Christianity had reached Wales in the early centuries through the work of missionaries such as David, Teilo, Cybi and Deiniol. One of these men would set up a small monastic church in a new district. Followers would come there to live, work and pray in a close-knit community — the 'clas'. The church of the 'clas' would be the mother-church for a wide area, and small chapels would spring up in convenient spots all over that area, like branches growing out of the trunk of a tree. In these chapels priests from the mother-church would hold services. But sometimes there would be so many worshippers in a chapel it would need a priest of its own; or perhaps a local lord would put up the money to provide one. Map A shows the scattered parish of Llanbadarn Fawr in Dyfed, with the mother-church surrounded by chapels which grew up into new churches with their own priests. Llanbadarn was the largest parish in Wales (over 50,000 hectares). A parish is the district cared for by one priest — usually a vicar or rector. But in many areas of Wales the parish churches grew as branches from one central tree.

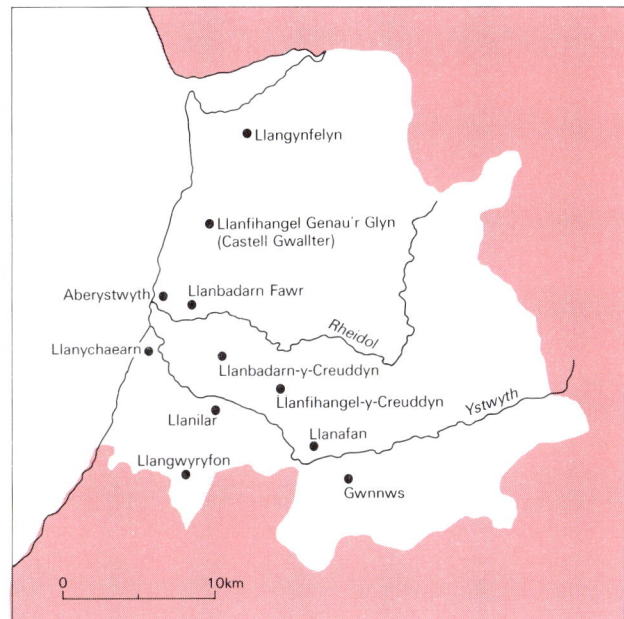

A A map of the parish of Llanbadarn Fawr. Why do you think the chapels were located as they were?

In the Norman lordships many knights paid for building churches and maintaining priests on their own lands. A long time passed before the boundaries between one parish and the next were settled, but the boundaries between dioceses were even more uncertain.

THE WELSH DIOCESES

The bishop is an important priest, because he has a very large area and many parishes under his control. The pattern of dioceses — districts controlled by bishops — had grown up slowly all over Europe through the centuries. But because Wales and the Celtic lands had been out of touch with the Church of Rome for a long time, their churches had developed different customs and ways of doing things. In Wales the dioceses grew up around important churches set up by some of the early missionaries — David at St David's, Teilo at Llandaff, Deiniol in Bangor and Kentigern at St Asaph. When the Normans tried to draw firm boundaries between them, a long dispute began between the bishops of St David's and Llandaff. They quarrelled about who should have control of the middle-ground between the two dioceses where both David and Teilo had been active. Extract B, which mentions the quarrel, comes from a history book written in the Middle Ages.

B There was a dispute between Bernard, bishop of St David's, and Urban, bishop of Llandav, on the right to parishes, which Urban had unlawfully **usurped**, the end of which was quashed. For after so many appeals to the Roman court, and so many expensive journeys, and so many disputes over so many years of the cause, at length it was settled by the death later at Rome of Urban ... for the pope ... by the right and justice of the claims of the bishop of St David's.

(William of Malmesbury, *Historia Novella*)

2. Do you think William favoured one side or the other in the dispute?

TWO DIOCESES IN CONFLICT

Shortly after taking up his new job as Archdeacon Gerald went around to collect his tithes. This was a kind of tax paid every year to the Church. On his return from the journey, and he had spent one night in a lonely church surrounded by armed enemies, bad news awaited him. He was told that the Bishop of St Asaph was hurrying south towards the Ceri district, which lay in the diocese of St David's and in Gerald's own archdeaconry. The Bishop intended to consecrate a new church there, and so claim the whole area as part of the St Asaph diocese. Gerald hurried there by the Sunday on which the Bishop was expected, galloping with his own priests and servants through the wooded vales of Powys. C

When he came face-to-face with the Bishop of St Asaph — a man who had been his friend when they were both students in Paris — Gerald insisted that the church was his. Imagine the scene: Gerald and his priests in their white vestments, carrying candles and a cross, and the Bishop in his fine robes with his shepherd's staff, both shouting at each other and threatening to **excommunicate** each other, while the superstitious local people watched in horror: D

D And when the Bishop swore that he meant to excommunicate them on the spot ... the Archdeacon asserted that he would pass sentence on them in like form. And when the Bishop ... began in a loud voice to excommunicate in general terms all enemies and adversaries of St Asaph, second bishop of the diocese of St Asaph] the Archdeacon in a still louder voice, together with his folk in the churchyard, excommunicated all those who presumed to appropriate or disturb the rights of St David; and looking back at the bells, which hung above their heads hard by, he ordered that they should all be rung ... for the shaming of their adversaries and for confirmation of his sentence. And when this was done, since the Welsh greatly dread such ringing of bells ... the Bishop and his men straight away broke off their sentence of excommunication and mounting their horses made off as fast as they could. But the people who had gathered from every side to behold this spectacle, raised a great shout behind them, after

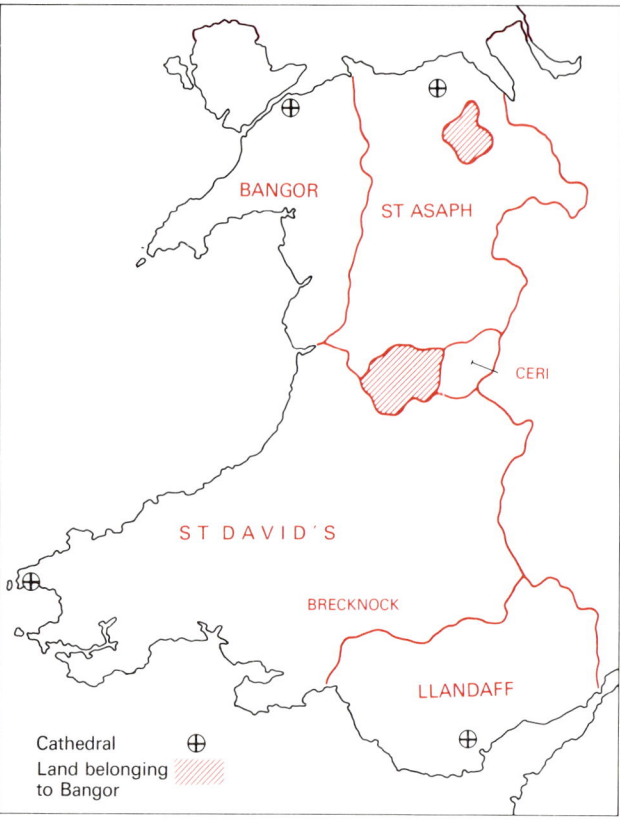

C A map of the Welsh dioceses.

their fashion, and pursued them as they fled with clods and sticks and stones.

(Gerald of Wales, *De Rebus a Se Gestis*, trans. H. E. Butler)

3. Why did a quarrel flare up between Gerald and the Bishop of St Asaph over the church of Ceri?
4. Draw a picture of the unusual events near the church of Ceri in 1175.

Before long Gerald was well-known at the court of King Henry II. When Gerald came to court, soon after the Ceri incident, the king asked him to tell the story in full — Henry had already heard it mentioned by someone else. Henry laughed and repeated the story to his court, and it caused great amusement.

On that same occasion, a matter came up which would concern Gerald for the rest of his life. Who was to be the next Bishop of St David's? Bishop David, Gerald's uncle, died in May 1176 and the bishops met in the presence of the king at Northampton to choose a new bishop.

This time, in 1176, they suggested the four Archdeacons — Gerald among them. Henry rejected all four and decided finally that Peter de Leia, the head of Wenlock **priory** near Shrewsbury, should be Bishop of St David's. E

E A bishop ordains a priest, as shown in an old manuscript.

CHOOSING A BISHOP

The method of choosing a bishop in the Roman Catholic Church had changed very little for centuries. According to ancient custom the Cathedral Canons — the leading clergymen — would draw up a list of the most deserving candidates. Then they would meet to elect one of them bishop. This was the normal method in the Catholic Church, but the freedom of the Canons to elect a bishop was limited. In most countries the Archbishop — the leading bishop — would present or consecrate the new bishop to his diocese. F

F The Archbishop of Canterbury consecrates a bishop.

In Wales the custom of the Celtic Church had been for the old bishop to name his successor before he died. The bishops, however, played an important part in the government of the country and the Norman kings wanted to choose their own men to be bishops.

5. How was a bishop usually chosen in the Middle Ages?

THE RIGHTS OF ST DAVID'S

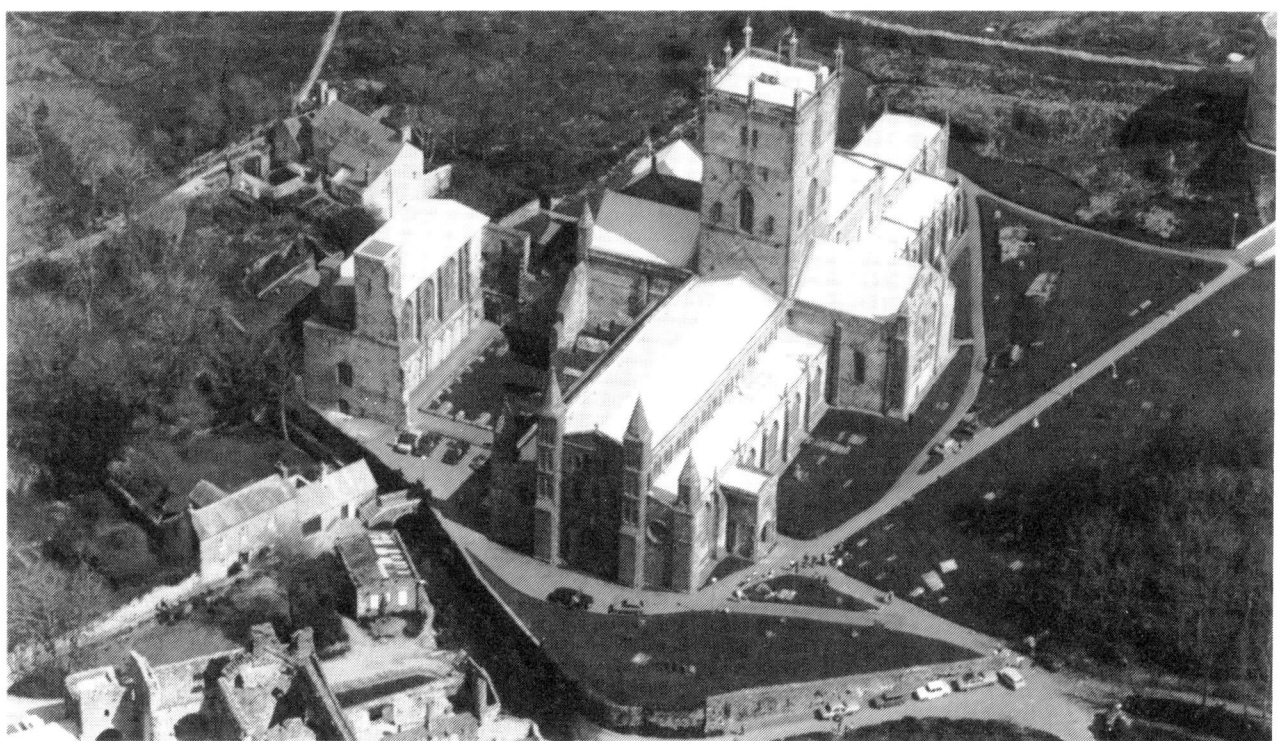

G St David's Cathedral.

In Gerald's opinion the Diocese of St David's was unlike any other diocese in Wales — or in England, for that matter. He saw it as the Mother-Church of all Wales. G What did this mean?

Gerald did not claim that St David's was the oldest church in Wales, but he was saying that it was the most important. After his election in 1199 Gerald said that St David's had been founded, or begun, by missionaries from Rome around the year AD 140. It was one of three **Archbishoprics** in Britain. Gerald came across this argument in the book *The Life of St David* which was written by the monk Rhigyfarch around 1090.

The Life of St David was a biography, or a life-story. Like most saints' lives it was written hundreds of years after the saint himself had died. The purpose of writing such a book was to show how good these saints were and also to prove a point that was important to the author. Rhigyfarch, who was the son of a Bishop of St David's, argued that David had been Archbishop of all Wales, and therefore all the later Bishops of St David's should be counted as Archbishops too. The story of how Gerald got involved in the arguments over St David's is told in more detail in *Gerald of Wales — 1*.

6. Why did Gerald regard St David's as a very special diocese?

7. What was *The Life of St David*?

After some (but not all) of the Canons of St David's — the senior priests of the diocese — had elected Gerald Bishop in 1199, the arguments became a blazing row. Hubert Walter, Archbishop of Canterbury, and the new king, John, refused to confirm his election, but the Canons of St David's stood their ground. The dispute went on for four years, and Gerald and his supporters appealed to the Pope Innocent III in Rome. He asked for his election to be confirmed and for St David's to be recognized as an Archbishopric, independent of Canterbury. This was the appeal St David's made: I

I We make known to your Holiness that we have at length in our Church canonically and with one accord elected our Archdeacon Master Giraldus after many demands, wherewith by the common consent of the clergy and all the people of this country we demanded him in preference to all others both from the King of England and from the Archbishop of Canterbury. Wherefore since the Archbishopric and the officers of the King, with violent intrusion against our election and our privileges, have desired to set over us a stranger, wholly ignorant of our native tongue and the customs of our country, and since from the oft refusal of our demands we found the will of the Archbishop wholly contrary to us ... we have therefore appealed to your protection and with one accord have sent to you, that you may confirm and consecrate him, our Elect [Gerald] ...

(Gerald of Wales, *De Rebus a Se Gestis*, trans. H. E. Butler)

H Llanddewi Brefi, where David preached.

During his time in Rome — and he went there three times — he got to know the Pope quite well. He gave Gerald every encouragement to search through the archives (old official papers) for letters and papers about the case. At times he seemed like a detective trying to rediscover forgotten facts and details, and some of the excitement he felt comes to life in his account.

J Castel Sant Angelo — the fortress where the Pope's archives and treasures were kept in Rome.

Gerald worked long and hard burrowing through the Pope's archives. J Then, one day, he found a letter written by Pope Eugenius III to Theobald, Archbishop of Canterbury, at the time of a previous claim for the status of an Archbishopric in 1147: K

K Our venerable brother Bernard, Bishop of St David's, having come before us, has claimed in person that the Church of St David was once Metropolitan [the centre of an Archbishopric], and has humbly demanded that we should restore it to that rank ... But since we desire that every Church and every ecclesiastic [priest] should keep the dignity that is their just due, we have fixed a day both for him and you on the feast of St Luke in the coming year, that we may then, both parties being present, discover the truth of the matter concerning the rank of the Church of St David and its liberty, and that we may, under God, decide what is just. Given at Meaux on the 29th day of June.

(Gerald of Wales, *De Iure et Statu Menuensis Ecclesiae*, trans. H. E. Butler)

Gerald was so excited when he saw the letter that he rushed to see a Cardinal who was the Pope's cousin and told him about it. He urged Gerald to go to the Pope that night: L

L So on the evening of the same day, about twilight, when he was entering the chamber to approach the Pope, the latter saluted him as Archbishop and called him to his side. Now Giraldus did not catch what the Pope had said, but Cardinal Ugolino, who was sitting on the other side of the Pope, said, 'Did you not hear by what name the Pope called you?' And Giraldus replied that he supposed the Pope had called him Archdeacon, after his wont, as indeed was his belief. But the Cardinal made answer, 'Nay, in truth, he saluted you as Archbishop.' And when he heard this, Giraldus prostrated himself at the feet of the Pope and kissed them, saying that by the grace of God and of the Pope these words were in truth prophetic, as they should be, proceeding from the mouth of so great a Pontiff [another name for the Pope]. And when the Pope went on to ask him whether he had found anything in the Register of Eugenius concerning the standing of the Church, he replied that he had, as indeed the Cardinal had already told the Pope. And when he gave him the writing, the Pope handed it to the Cardinal and bade him read it aloud. And when it had been read, the Pope replied that he was well pleased with it and granted the Archdeacon the Commission to inquire into the standing of the Church which he had desired ...

(Gerald of Wales, *De Iure et Statu Menuensis Ecclesiae*, trans. H. E. Butler)

8. What evidence had Gerald found in Rome that strengthened the case in favour of St David's?

DEFEAT AND DISAPPOINTMENT

So now it seemed as if Gerald's campaign to win recognition for St David's as an Archbishopric was on the brink of success. But there were difficulties ahead. By the spring of 1203, nearly five years after the death of the previous Bishop, Gerald was facing total defeat. The hopes of St David's were shattered. How could he have failed when all seemed to be going so well and even the Pope sympathized with his case?

Gerald's case had serious weaknesses. First, he had not been elected by all the Canons of St David's — only by three of them. Secondly, the previous Bishops at St David's had accepted the leadership of the Archbishop of Canterbury for years. The Pope never actually turned down St David's claim to be independent. What he did say firmly in 1203 was that Gerald had not been elected fairly as Bishop. Eventually Geoffrey of Henlaw, the head of Llanthony Priory, was elected Bishop of St David's.

Gerald had challenged not only the Archbishop of Canterbury and the entire English Church, but also the king himself. John knew as well as anyone that an independent Church in Wales would strengthen the ambitions of princes like Llywelyn ap Iorwerth in Gwynedd to be independent of England. The Church and the government put all the pressure they could on the canons of St David's to change their minds while Gerald was away in Rome. On his first return visit, and even more so on his second visit, he sensed that the support of the Canons was flagging, old friends backing down and ready to obey Canterbury and the king.

9. Why did the St David's campaign fail in the end?

In 1215 — when King John was quarrelling with his warlike barons — the Canons of St David's again asked Gerald to be their Bishop. He refused, but he was glad that a Welshman was elected this time — Iorwerth, the Abbot of Talley. Gerald was probably not fully satisfied — he was a difficult man to please at the best of times. He complained that Iorwerth was too ready to put up with slack discipline on the part of the Welsh priests, but he was less critical of Iorwerth than of the two Bishops before him. Gerald died in Lincoln in 1223, among his books and his memories of an eventful life.

10. Why do you think the Church was so powerful in the age of Gerald?

11. Why did the dioceses of Wales develop as they did?

12. Why might Gerald have been pleased when a new Bishop was elected at St David's in 1215?

13. Look at the staffs, or sticks, held by the Bishop and Archbishop in pictures E and F. What is unusual about their design, and why were staffs of this sort part of the dress and equipment of every Archbishop and Bishop?

14. What words would you use to describe Gerald's character, judging from what you have read about him and from his own words? List his good points and his bad points.

7. GLOSSARY

Archbishopric — a diocese which is the leader of a group of other dioceses.

Archdeacon — an important priest in the Church, second in rank to a Bishop, and with a wide area in his care.

Charter — an official document listing special privileges granted to someone by an important person.

Confections — sweet foods.

Diocese — a district whose churches are all controlled by a single bishop.

Excommunicate — to exclude someone from membership and from the services of the Church.

Frontier — land on the border between one state or one way of life and another, or marking the limit of military conquest.

Homage — promising loyalty to a lord or king and accepting their leadership.

Liberate — to free or to rescue someone.

Outlaw — a person outside law-abiding society, a criminal on the run.

Priory — a monastic house ruled by a Prior.

Profession — the work a person does.

Psalter — a book of Psalms, or songs from the Old Testament.

Usurp — to take over a title, an important job or some property without having any legal right to it.